Yellow Umbrella Books are published by Capstone Press
151 Good Counsel Drive, P.O. Box 669, Mankato, Minnesota 56002
http://www.capstone-press.com

Library of Congress Cataloging-in-Publication Data
Trumbauer, Lisa, 1963–
   Animal ears/by Lisa Trumbauer; consulting editor, Gail Saunders-Smith.
   p. cm.
   Includes index.
   ISBN 0-7368-0723-3
   1. Ear—Juvenile literature. [1. Ear. 2. Hearing. 3. Senses and sensation. 4. Animals.]
I. Saunders-Smith, Gail. II. Title.
QL948.T78   2001
573.8'9—dc21   00-036479

   Summary: Describes the ears of many types of animals and tells how the animals use
   their ears.

Editorial Credits:
Susan Evento, Managing Editor/Product Development; Elizabeth Jaffe, Senior Editor;
   Charles Hunt, Designer; Kimberly Danger and Heidi Schoof, Photo Researchers

Photo Credits:
Cover: Thomas Kitchin/TOM STACK & ASSOCIATES; Title Page: Cheryl Ertelt (top left),
James Rowan (bottom left), Robert McCaw (top right), Brian Parker/TOM STACK &
ASSOCIATES (bottom right); Page 2: Photo Network/Cynthia Salter; Page 3: Photo
Network/Cynthia Salter (top left), Mary Clay/Cole Photo (top right), Index Stock Imagery
(bottom); Page 4: Robert McCaw; Page 5: Thomas Kitchin/TOM STACK & ASSOCIATES; Page
6: Visuals Unlimited/Ken Lucas; Page 7: Visuals Unlimited/Steve Maslowski; Page 8: Photo
Network/Mark Newman; Page 9: Mark Newman; Page 10: Joe McDonald/TOM STACK &
ASSOCIATES; Page 11: Index Stock Imagery; Page 12: Index Stock Imagery; Page 13: Index
Stock Imagery and/Scott Kerrigan; Page 14: Bill Beatty; Page 15: Index Stock Imagery (top),
Robert McCaw (bottom); Page 16: Robert McCaw (top left), Root Resources/Mary Root (top
right), Photo Network/Mark Newman (bottom)

1 2 3 4 5 6 06 05 04 03 02 01

Animal Ears

by Lisa Trumbauer

Consulting Editor: Gail Saunders-Smith, Ph.D.
Consultants: Claudine Jellison and
Patricia Williams, Reading Recovery Teachers
Content Consultant: Judi Adler, Sweetbay Newfoundlands

Yellow Umbrella Books

an imprint of Capstone Press
Mankato, Minnesota

All animals have ears.
People have ears.
Ears help us hear.

Some ears are big.

Some ears are small.

Some ears are hard to see at all.

Look at the big ears
on these elephants.
Big ears help elephants
hear well.

An elephant can move its ears back and forth, like a fan.
Its ears keep the elephant cool.

This fox lives in the desert.
Its big ears let out body heat
to keep the fox cool.
Its big ears help it hear well too.

This rabbit also has big ears.
Do you think its ears
keep it cool?
Do you think its ears
help it hear well?
Yes!

A zebra's ears move
to hear sounds.
A zebra can hear
if an enemy is near.

Other animals move their ears
to find food.
A lioness listens to hear
if the animals she hunts are near.

A bat uses its big ears to find
food. A bat makes high sounds.
The sounds bounce off things
to make echoes.
The bat can hear and follow the
echoes to find insects to eat.

This is an otter.

It can close its small round ears
to keep out water when it swims.

Some ears seem to show feelings.
Look at the ears on these dogs.
This dog seems happy.

This dog seems sad.

How do their ears look different?

Not all ears are easy to see.
You can see the ears
on a baby bird.
But this grown-up bird
has feathers that hide its ears.

Can you see the ear on this frog?
It is shaped like a circle.

Can you see the ear on this snake?
No. It is inside the snake's body.

All animals have ears.

Some ears
are big.

Some ears
are small.

And some are hard to see at all!

Words to Know/Index

desert—a dry, sandy place with few or no plants; very little rain falls in a desert; page 6

different—not the same; page 13

echo—a sound that repeats when sound waves bounce back from a surface; page 10

elephant—a very large mammal with thick gray or brown skin, two tusks, and a long trunk; pages 4, 5

enemy—a person, a group, or an animal that does not like another; enemies may fight each other page 8

hunt—to chase and kill animals for food; page 9

insect—a small animal with a hard outer shell, six legs, and three body parts; some insects have two pairs of wings; page 10

lioness—a female lion; lions are large, brown wildcats found in Africa and southern Asia; page 9

otter—a furry mammal with a long body, a long tail, and webbed feet; otters use their feet to swim; page 11

zebra—a mammal of Africa with dark stripes on a white or tan body; zebras are related to horses; page 8

Word count: 301
Early Intervention Levels: 13-16